# TOM BRADY

By Jeff Savage

AMAZING ATHLETES

Lerner Publications Company • Minneapolis

*For Bailey Savage—as cool as Tom Brady*

Lerner Publications Company
A division of Lerner Publishing Group, Inc.
241 First Avenue North
Minneapolis, Minnesota 55401 U.S.A.

Website address: www.lernerbooks.com

Library of Congress Cataloging-in-Publication Data

Savage, Jeff, 1961–
Tom Brady / by Jeff Savage.
 p.   cm. — (Amazing athletes)
Includes index.
ISBN 13: 978–0–8225–2948–4 (lib. bdg. : alk. paper)
ISBN 10: 0–8225–2948–3 (lib. bdg. : alk. paper)
1. Brady, Tom, 1977– —Juvenile literature. 2. Football players—United States—Biography—Juvenile literature. I. Title. II. Series.
GV939.B685S38 2006
796.332'092—dc22                                        2005002921

Manufactured in the United States of America
 5 6 7 8 9 – DP – 12 11 10 09 08 07

# TABLE OF CONTENTS

New England Patriot Tom Brady looks tense during the 2004 Super Bowl against the Carolina Panthers.

# SUPER HERO

Tom Brady had every reason to be nervous. Near the end of the 2004 **Super Bowl**, Tom's New England Patriots were trailing the Carolina Panthers by one point, 22–21. The Patriots hadn't been behind in a game in more than two months. Tom had just watched Panthers **quarterback** Jake Delhomme throw an 85-yard **touchdown** pass to **wide receiver** Muhsin Muhammad. This was the longest touchdown pass in Super Bowl history.

Panthers' wide receiver Muhsin Muhammad makes the catch. The pass resulted in an 85-yard touchdown.

Tom sets his feet to throw a pass.

But Tom stayed calm. He was a cool quarterback, and his teammates knew it. Tom had shocked the world two years earlier. In the 2002 Super Bowl, he had led his team to a dramatic win in the last few seconds against the St. Louis Rams. Could he do it again?

Tom zipped smart passes to lead his team down the field. From the one-yard line, he flicked a pass to Mike Vrabel for the go-ahead score. The Patriots added a **two-point conversion** for a 29–22 lead. Only 2:55 was left in the game. Tom was the hero again. Or was he?

The Panthers came back. They drove 80 yards in seven plays to tie the game with 1:08 remaining.

Mike Vrabel (number 50) scoots around Carolina defender Deon Grant (number 27). Vrabel's effort helped the Patriots take the lead.

Patriots' wide receiver Deion Branch escapes the clutches of Ricky Manning. Branch sped up the field to get the Patriots within field-goal range.

Tom had to get his team going yet again. He completed a short pass and then another. Soon the Patriots reached the Carolina 40-yard line. Just 14 seconds were left on the clock. Tom had time for one more smart play. He dodged **defenders** and fired a pass to Deion Branch. The wide receiver caught it and sped down the sideline for 17 yards. The Patriots were close enough to kick a **field goal**.

Kicker Adam Vinatieri lined up for the kick. He booted the ball high and through the **uprights**. The Patriots won the game, 32–29. "You dream about playing football," said Tom. "But you don't dream about winning Super Bowls like this. The way it ended is just incredible." The question became, could Tom keep on pace to win in 2005?

Tom holds up the Super Bowl trophy, as his teammates celebrate around him.

Tom grew up near San Francisco in the 1980s. At that time, San Francisco quarterback Joe Montana *(above)* was at the top of his game.

# LEARNING TO COMPETE

Tom was born August 3, 1977. He was the fourth child of Tom Sr. and Galynn Brady. The Bradys lived in San Mateo, a city near San Francisco, California. Tom was the baby brother to three sisters—Maureen, Julie, and Nancy. The entire family was crazy about sports.

Tom's boyhood hero was Joe Montana. During the 1980s, Montana was the Super Bowl-winning quarterback of the San Francisco 49ers. Just like Montana, Tom was not especially big or fast. But he loved to play sports. By age six, Tom was challenging older boys to run races.

Tom hated to lose. And sometimes he was not a good sport about losing. He threw his video game controller at the TV. He smashed his tennis racket on the court. "It got to where nobody wanted to play with me," he said.

In 1991, when Tom was fourteen, he started going to Junipero Serra High School. By this time, he'd learned to control his emotions. Serra High was known for its sports programs. Tom played catcher on the school's baseball team. But football was Tom's favorite sport.

Tom *(left)* stretches to tag out a player during a baseball game at Serra High.

In addition to daily practice, Tom created a tough workout program to stay in shape. Tom threw for nearly 4,000 yards and 31 touchdowns during high school. His skills drew the attention of more than 75 colleges around the country.

Tom was also a talented baseball player. The Montreal Expos picked him in the 1995 baseball draft. But Tom chose to go to college and play football.

# WAITING HIS TURN

In 1995, at age seventeen, Tom sorted through his **scholarship** offers. He chose the University of Michigan, whose team name is the Wolverines. He moved away from home and became Michigan's **third-string** quarterback. College was fun for Tom, but he didn't get to play his first two years. He grew frustrated.

"I turned into a whiner," Tom admitted. He told his coach, Lloyd Carr, that he wanted to transfer to the University of California. Coach Carr convinced Tom not to give up. "Just put everything else out of your mind and worry about making yourself better," he told his young player.

Tom did as his coach told him. In 1998, in his third year, he became the team's starting quarterback. Over the next two years, Tom guided the Wolverines to a record of 20 wins and 5 losses. Tom's final college pass was a game-winning touchdown. It earned the Wolverines a dramatic 35–34 win over the University of Alabama in the Orange Bowl.

Tom dives past a defender to make a touchdown during a game in his last year at the University of Michigan.

The New England Patriots picked Tom in 2000. He became the backup quarterback to their veteran quarterback Drew Bledsoe *(above)*.

But during the 2000 National Football League (NFL) **Draft**, coaches were not impressed. Tom wasn't drafted until the New England Patriots took him in the sixth round. He was very disappointed.

He joined the New England Patriots as a **rookie** quarterback. He would back up the team's **veteran** quarterback Drew Bledsoe.

In the 2000 season, Tom watched the Patriots finish last in their **division**. For the year, he completed just one pass for six yards. But Tom didn't pout. Instead, he worked harder. He practiced his **footwork** and memorized the team's **playbook**.

The 2001 season began badly. The Patriots lost their first two games. During the second loss, Bledsoe suffered a serious chest injury. He would be out for the season. Coach Belichick told Tom he was going to start the third game.

Patriots' head coach Bill Belichick noticed Tom squeezed the ball with a hard grip. This grip allowed him to throw a tight spiral. But this way of throwing also meant he didn't throw the ball very far. Tight spirals tend to be more on target. Tom liked being an accurate passer rather than a long passer.

Snow was a factor in one famous playoff game against the Oakland Raiders. Slipping and sliding, Tom narrowly escapes a bunch of defenders to get a touchdown.

# SEIZING THE MOMENT

Tom seized the chance. He was careful and smart. In fact, he didn't throw an **interception** in his first 162 **pass attempts**. This was an NFL record. He led the Patriots to 11 wins in 14 games and into the **playoffs**.

In the first playoff game, New England played the Oakland Raiders at the Patriots' stadium in Foxboro, Massachusetts. It was January 2002, and snow blanketed the field. Playing was tough. At the end of the fourth quarter, the Patriots tied the game with a field goal. The game went into **overtime.** Tom marched his team close enough for the kicker to make another field goal and win the game.

Patriots' kicker Adam Vinatieri raises his fist in celebration. He'd just kicked a field goal to defeat the Raiders in the playoffs.

A week later, the Patriots upset the Pittsburgh Steelers to reach the Super Bowl. Everyone was asking, who is this kid Tom Brady?

The Patriots weren't favored to win the Super Bowl. They'd be playing the high-powered St. Louis Rams.

One by one, the Rams' major players ran onto the field. The Patriots came out in one big group—as a team. This was the way they wanted to play.

Tom kept his cool in the game. The Patriots carried a 17–3 lead into the fourth quarter. But the Rams stormed back to tie the game.

Before playing in the Super Bowl in 2002, some of Tom's teammates paced the locker room. Others studied the game plan. What was Tom doing? He was stretched out on the floor taking a nap!

Tom gets out of trouble during Super Bowl XXXVI against the St. Louis Rams.

The Patriots had no timeouts left. Only 1:21 was left on the clock. Tom dodged defenders and completed a pass. Then he completed another. Calmly, he hurried his team. With three more passes, he moved the Patriots to the Rams' 30-yard line.

With seven seconds left on the clock, Adam Vinatieri *(left)* came through with a 48-yard field goal. Tom was the youngest quarterback to win a Super Bowl. He was also the youngest MVP.

Seven seconds remained. Vinatieri lined up for a field goal. The ball sailed through the uprights for a stunning victory! Tom was named the game's most valuable player (MVP). "Incredible," said Tom. "That's why you keep working hard."

Tom's next stop after his win was a trip to Disney World in Florida!

# CALIFORNIA COOL

Tom's life changed suddenly. As the game's MVP, he was flown to Disney World. He returned to Boston, Massachusetts, for the team's victory parade. Then he flew to Hawaii to play in the **Pro Bowl**.

He played golf with football great Dan Marino. He hung out with baseball stars Barry Bonds and Willie Mays. He got so many phone calls that he had to change his telephone number—three times. Tom admitted that all the attention was wearing him out.

At the same time, Bledsoe was traded. The Patriots had become Tom's team. He finished the

Tom *(left)* traded golf tips with former Miami Dolphins quarterback Dan Marino.

Tom earned the MVP award again in 2004 against the Carolina Panthers in Super Bowl XXXVIII.

2002 season with more touchdown passes than any other quarterback. But the Patriots finished with a 9–7 record and missed the playoffs. Tom was determined not to let that happen again.

New England opened the 2003 season with a 31–0 loss to the Buffalo Bills. Then the Patriots won 17 of their next 18 games. They ended their season with their second Super Bowl victory in three years. Tom was an easy choice for Super Bowl MVP again.

The Patriots kept up their winning pace in the 2004 season. In the playoffs, Tom got the Patriots into the **end zone** time after time. The team beat the Indianapolis Colts and the Pittsburgh Steelers. Tom didn't throw any interceptions.

Tom talks with Steelers' rookie quarterback Ben Rothlisberger. Tom's team had just beaten the Steelers in the playoffs.

Tom kept control of his team during Super Bowl XXXIX in 2005. The Patriots have won three out of the last four Super Bowls.

In the Super Bowl, the Patriots defeated the Philadelphia Eagles, 24–21. The Patriots had won their third championship in four years. Once again, Tom didn't throw an interception. In five years, Tom had played in nine playoff games. He'd won all nine. After the season, the Patriots gave Tom a new six-year contract worth $60 million.

Tom had another great season in 2005. But despite his solid play, Tom's streak of playoff victories came to an end. The Patriots lost to the Denver Broncos in a 2005 divisional playoff game, 27–13. The 2006 season also ended poorly for the Patriots with a 38–34 loss to the Colts in the playoffs.

Even Joe Montana hadn't won two Super Bowl MVP awards within his first five years in the NFL.

Because of his many Super Bowl wins, Tom has been compared to Joe Montana, his boyhood idol. Montana's nickname was Joe Cool. Tom's nickname is California Cool. Like Montana, Tom is calm when the game is on the line. But Montana won four Super Bowls. Could Tom match that? He's giving it his best shot!

# Selected Career Highlights

**2006**   Tied for fourth in the NFL with 24 touchdown passes

**2005**   Named *Sports Illustrated*'s Sportsman of the Year
Named to the Pro Bowl for third time
Threw 100th career regular season touchdown pass

**2004**   Won Super Bowl title for third time
Completed five touchdowns with no interceptions in three
  playoff games
Improved all-time playoff record to 9–0
Was named to the Pro Bowl

**2003**   Won Super Bowl title and game's MVP award for second time
Finished third in the voting as overall league MVP

**2002**   Led NFL quarterbacks with 28 touchdown passes

**2001**   Won Super Bowl title and named game's MVP
Set Patriots playoff game records for most pass
  attempts (52), most completions (32), and
  most yards passing (312) in a game against
  the Oakland Raiders
Completed the most passes of any
  Patriot in team history
Named to the Pro Bowl in his first
  season as a starter

**1999**   All-Big Ten Conference second-
  team selection

**1998**   All-Big Ten Conference honorable
  mention
All-Big Ten Academic team
Set University of Michigan record for most
  pass attempts (350) and completions (214)
  in a season

**1995**   Junipero Serra High School team
  MVP
Drafted in 18th round as a
  catcher by Montreal Expos
  baseball team

# Glossary

**defender:** a player whose job is to try to stop the other team from scoring points

**division:** within the NFL, one of four sets of teams in each conference. The Patriots are part of the Eastern Division of the American Football Conference.

**draft:** a yearly event in which all professional teams in a sport are given the chance to pick new players from a selected group. Most of the players in the group have played their sport in college.

**end zone:** the area beyond the goal line at either end of the field. To score, a team tries to get the ball into the other team's end zone.

**field goal:** a successful kick over the U-shaped upright poles on the defending team's end of the field. A field goal is worth three points.

**footwork:** the steps a quarterback takes before throwing or handing off the ball

**interception:** a pass that is caught by a person on the defense. An interception results in the opposing team getting control of the ball.

**overtime:** in NFL rules, an extra fifteen minutes played when the teams are tied. The first team to score wins.

**pass attempts:** the number of passes a quarterback throws in a game or a season

**playbook:** a book that describes plays a team will use in games

**playoffs:** a series of contests played after the regular season has ended

**Pro Bowl:** a game played after each season between the stars of the American Football Conference and the National Football Conference

**quarterback:** in football, the person who throws or hands off the ball

**rookie:** a player who is playing his or her first season

**scholarship:** money awarded to a student to pay for the cost of attending college

**Super Bowl:** The final game of each season between the champions of the American Football Conference and the National Football Conference. The winner of the Super Bowl is that season's NFL champion.

**third-string:** the name given to the third player at a certain position. The first-string player is the starting player. The second-string player would replace the first-string player and so on.

**touchdown:** a score in which the team with the ball crosses the other team's goal line. A touchdown is worth six points.

**two-point conversion:** a scoring play made immediately after a touchdown that is worth two points. A team can get the two points by running or passing the ball into the opponent's end zone on one play starting from the opponent's two-yard line.

**uprights:** The two posts on the ends of the crossbar of a goalpost. A field-goal kick between the uprights is worth three points.

**veteran:** a player who has played for a number of years

**wide receiver:** a player who catches passes, mainly for a big gain

# Further Reading & Websites

Cafardo, Nick. *The Impossible Team: The Worst to First Patriots Super Bowl Season.* Chicago: Triumph Books, 2002.

Lazenby, Roland, and Bob Schron. *Tom Brady: Sudden Glory.* Chicago: Triumph Books, 2002.

Stewart, Mark. *Tom Brady: Heart of the Huddle.* Brookfield, CT: Millbrook Press, 2003.

New England Patriots
http://www.patriots.com
The official website of the New England Patriots.

Official NFL Site
http://www.nfl.com
The official National Football League website provides fans with game action, biographies of players, and information about football.

*Sports Illustrated for Kids*
http://www.sikids.com
The *Sports Illustrated for Kids* website covers all sports, including football.

# Index

# Photo Acknowledgments

Photographs are used with the permission of: © John Zich/New
Sport/CORBIS, p. 4; © Brian Bahr/Getty Images, p. 5; © SportsChrome
East/West, Tom DiPace, p. 6; © PIERRE DUCHARME/Reuters/CORBIS, p. 7;
© Jeff Gross/Getty Images, p. 8; SportsChrome East/West, Rob Tringali, p. 9;
© John McDonough/Icon SMI, p. 10; Courtesy of Russ Bertetta, Junipero
Serra High School, p. 12; © Reuters/CORBIS, pp. 15, 16, 18, 19, 21, 22 (left
and right); © CHARLES W. LUZIER/Reuters/CORBIS, p. 23; © Steven Dunn/
Getty Images, p. 24; © Win McNamee/Reuters/CORBIS, p. 25; © Jay Drowns/
Sporting News/ZUMA Press, p. 26; © Jeff Lewis/Icon SMI, p. 27; © Kevin
Reece/Icon SMI/ZUMA Press, p. 29.

Cover: © Kevin Reece/Icon SMI/ZUMA Press.